THE KANGAROOS

BY
WILLIAM R. SANFORD
CARL R. GREEN

EDITED BY
DR. HOWARD SCHROEDER
Professor in Reading and Language Arts
Dept. of Elementary Education
Mankato State University

PRODUCED AND DESIGNED BY
BAKER STREET PRODUCTIONS
Mankato, MN

CRESTWOOD HOUSE
Mankato, Minnesota

LIBRARY OF CONGRESS CATALOGING IN PUBLICATION DATA

Sanford, William R. (William Reynolds)
  The kangaroo.

(Wildlife, habits & habitat)
Includes index.
SUMMARY: Discusses kangaroos, their habits, habitat, life cycle, desirability to man, and problems they face in staying alive.
  1. Kangaroos--Juvenile literature. (1. Kangaroos.) I. Green, Carl R. II. Schroeder, Howard. III. Baker Street Productions. IV. Title. V. Series.
QL737.M35S26   1987   599.2   86-32881
ISBN 0-89686-322-0

International Standard Book Number:	Library of Congress Catalog Card Number:
Library Binding 0-89686-322-0	86-32881

ILLUSTRATION CREDITS:

Cover Photo: John Cancalosi/Tom Stack & Associates
Stephen J. Krasemann: 5, 9, 10, 17, 18, 20, 26, 29, 33, 37, 41
John Cancalosi/Tom Stack & Associates: 6, 24-25, 30, 38, 45
Bob Williams: 13
M.P. Kahl/DRK Photo: 14, 34

Copyright© 1987 by Crestwood House, Inc. All rights reserved. No part of this book may be reproduced in any form without written permission from the publisher, except for brief passages included in a review. Printed in the United States of America.

Hwy. 66 South, Box 3427
Mankato, MN 56002-3427

TABLE OF CONTENTS

Introduction: 4
Chapter I: 8
   A large and varied family
   The largest of all marsupials
   Legs and tail made for leaping
   An animal designed for eating grass
   Senses alert to danger
   Low in brainpower
Chapter II: 16
   Life in the mob
   Hungry grazers, world-class leapers
   The kangaroo's enemies
   Timid until cornered
Chapter III: 23
   A fight with no holds barred
   A thimble-sized joey
   Life in the pouch
   A first look at the world
   Growing up
   On her own
Chapter IV: 35
   A taste for "hopping mutton"
   The threat of extinction
   The killing goes on
Chapter V: 40
   Hunters go where the roos are
   A hard way to make a living
   The hunt begins
   It's time for a cup of tea
Map 46
Index/Glossary 47

INTRODUCTION:

"Why can't school be like this everyday?" Sally asked.

Mr. Olson smiled at Sally and the rest of his noisy class. "I thought you'd like this field trip to the zoo," he said. "Now, hurry into the animal nursery. Dr. Penner told me that she has something special to show you."

Inside the nursery, a woman in a lab coat was standing by a glass-walled cage. "If you'll be very quiet, I think the joey will poke its head out of Kanga's pouch," Dr. Penner said.

Sally grabbed Benny's arm. "It's a kangaroo!" she whispered. "She must be five feet (1.5 m) tall! But what's a joey?"

"A joey is a young kangaroo," Dr. Penner replied.

Just then, a small head popped out of the pouch on Kanga's stomach. "Hey," Sally laughed, "that's handy! All mothers should have a big pocket like that for carrying their babies."

Claudia pushed in closer. "Why do kangaroos have pouches?" she asked. "Bears and tigers don't carry their babies that way."

"Bears and tigers are placental mammals," Dr. Penner told the class. "An unborn bear cub spends its first months inside its mother. A special sack called a

A baby kangaroo, called a joey, peeks out of its mother's pouch.

placenta provides the cub with all the food and oxygen it needs to grow. By the time it's born, the bear is big enough and strong enough to survive."

Tommy's hand shot up. "I bet you're going to tell us that kangaroos don't have a placenta," he said.

"That's right," Dr. Penner said with a smile. "Mammals like the kangaroo are called marsupials. When they're born, marsupials are hardly developed at all. They live in the pouch until they're big enough to take care of themselves."

"I know that kangaroos come from Australia," Conrad said. "Do marsupials live anywhere else?"

A baby marsupial will stay in its mother's pouch until it can take care of itself. These are grey kangaroos.

"North America's only marsupial is the opossum," Mr. Olson answered. "But of the 250 marsupials still living, Australia and the nearby islands have 170. That's because the continent of Australia broke away from Asia a long time ago. The marsupials developed without being forced to compete with the more advanced placental mammals."

"In fact," Dr. Penner added, "naturalists call Australia 'the land of living fossils.' Animals such as the kangaroo, the duckbill platypus, and the bandikoot live only in Australia."

Mr. Olson looked at his watch. "It's almost time for the bus," he said. "There's time for one more question."

"Does Australia have any placental mammals?" Rose asked.

"Except for a few bats and mice, the marsupial was king for thousands of years," Dr. Penner replied. "Humans added the other placental mammals to Australia's animal population. The first was a wild dog known as the dingo. The first Australians—the aborigines—brought the ancestor of the dingo with them about thirty thousand years ago."

Everyone in the class waved to Kanga as they left. Back on the bus, Mr. Olson quieted them down. "Okay, gang," he said. "What do you say to a unit on marsupials next week?"

Sally and Benny led the cheers. "I'll write my report on the kangaroo," Sally promised.

CHAPTER ONE:

Marsupials are rare in most places, but not in Australia. The "land down under" is home to more than a hundred million kangaroos. Over hundreds of centuries, these big-footed leapers have developed into forty-seven different species. They range in size from eight-foot (2.4 m) red kangaroos to sixteen-inch (41 cm) rat kangaroos. The different species live in habitats that range from grassy plains to swamps to rocky hillsides.

A large and varied family

All kangaroos belong to the families *Macropus* and *Megaleia*. *Macropus* is a good family name, for it comes from the Latin word for "long foot." With a family this large, it's not surprising that people call the various kangaroos by different names. Generally, the name "kangaroo" belongs to the largest members of the family. The heavier, shorter hill-climbers are known as wallaroos. Wallabies are smaller yet, and rat kangaroos are the smallest of all.

The wallaroo *(Macropus robustus)* is also called the euro in some areas. Wallaroos have long, shaggy fur and a stocky build. They range in color from dark grey to reddish-brown. These kangaroos live everywhere in Australia except in the northern forests and the far southwest. Like the camel, wallaroos can go for many days without water.

The red kangaroo *(Macropus rufus)* is known as the plains kangaroo because of its habitat. Males are also called red fliers because of their color. The reds are the largest of all kangaroos. Most males are reddish in color on their back and sides, but others may be red-and-grey, or entirely grey. The females are usually blue-

Red kangaroos are the largest members of the kangaroo family.

grey in color, and are sometimes called blue fliers. Red kangaroos are found mostly in the vast grassy plains of central Australia.

The kangaroo most often seen in zoos is the grey kangaroo *(Macropus giganteus)*. The grey is a little smaller than the red, both in height and in the length of its hind legs. The greys from inland areas have thick, short fur. They're usually grey-brown, with lighter areas on the legs and darker areas at the tip of their paws and tail. Greys from the east coastal region have longer, silvery-grey fur. Australians sometimes speak of the grey as the forester because of its woodland habitat.

Australians often call the grey kangaroo the "forester" because of its woodland habitat.

The largest of all marsupials

An adult grey kangaroo often measures seven feet (2.1 m) from the tip of its nose to the tip of its tail. The same animal may weigh two hundred pounds (91 kg). The record for height is held by a kangaroo that measured nine feet, seven inches (2.87 m). In its usual crouching position, however, a kangaroo is four to five feet tall (1.2 m to 1.5 m). If it hears a sudden noise, the kangaroo will stretch to its full height while it listens.

Kangaroos grow to full size in seven or eight years. Males are larger and heavier than females, especially through the shoulders. Unlike most animals, kangaroos continue to grow for as long as they live. That can be up to twenty years, but most kangaroos live only seven or eight years. About forty percent of the joeys die before they're a year old.

Legs and tail made for leaping

Kangaroos are four-legged animals, but the front and back legs do very different jobs. The forelegs measure about two feet (61 cm) from shoulder to paw. Each paw has four toes that end in sharp claws. The kangaroo uses its forelegs for support when it leans forward to eat and when it's moving slowly. It also uses its forearms to hold an enemy or to "box" with another kangaroo.

By contrast, up to three-fourths of a kangaroo's weight is located in its hind legs. When frightened, these strong legs and long feet transform the clumsy four-legged creature into a graceful, two-legged flyer. When running, a kangaroo bounds along in leaps that leave it airborne seventy percent of the time! If it can't leap away from danger, the kangaroo can deliver a powerful karate kick with its hind legs.

The kangaroo's hind foot is even more unusual. The back feet of adult greys range from twelve to eighteen inches (30 to 45 cm) in length. These long, narrow feet have five toes, each tipped with a claw. The middle toe is much bigger than the others. It has a long, sharp claw that's useful in a fight. The two smallest toes are located on the side of each rear foot. The kangaroo uses them to scratch itself and clean its fur.

A six-foot (1.8 m) kangaroo is more than one-half tail. The thick, well-muscled tail, which is about four feet (1.2 m) long, helps support the animal when it's sitting upright. It also gives the kangaroo a "five-footed" gait. When it's grazing, for example, a kangaroo balances on its tail and forepaws as it pushes off with its hind legs. For high speed movement, the kangaroo switches to a two-footed gait. With its tail held straight back, it leaps forward off its hind legs. The tail provides balance and also serves as a rudder. A slight movement to left or right steers the kangaroo in a new direction.

An animal designed for eating grass

The shape of a kangaroo's head looks a bit like the head of a sheep or deer. The long jaw is designed for cutting and chewing the grasses that make up the biggest part of a kangaroo's diet. Two sharp cutting teeth at the front of the lower jaw clamp the grass against a pad in the upper jaw. A sharp jerk of the kangaroo's head then snaps off each tasty mouthful. In forest areas, they also eat vines and small trees.

The kangaroo's grinding teeth (molars) lie about two inches (5 cm) behind its front teeth. Each jaw has four or five molars on a side. The molars fall out when they're worn down by constant chewing. The remaining

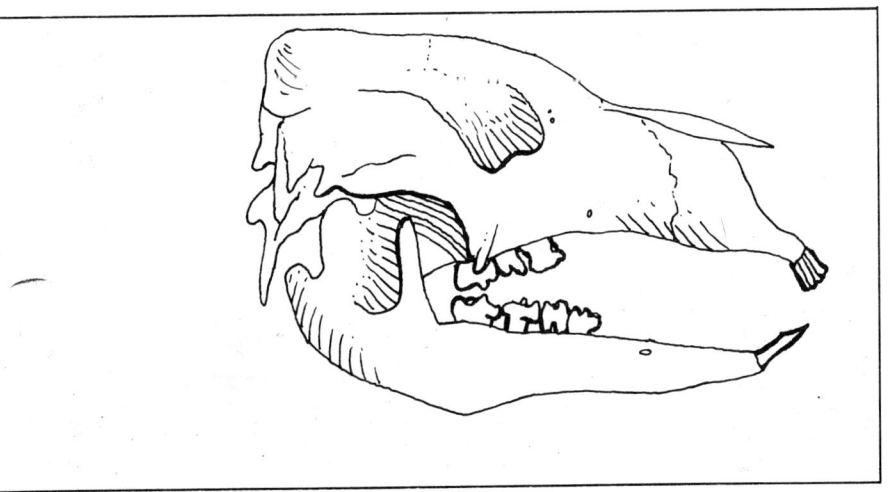

Cutting teeth in front, and grinding teeth in the back, equip a kangaroo for eating grass.

molars move forward to replace the missing teeth. A kangaroo doesn't grow new molars to replace those that are lost, however. Left without molars for chewing, an old kangaroo will starve to death.

Digestion takes place in the kangaroo's stomach, which has several chambers. Bacteria and strong acids break down the well-chewed grasses and extract the food value. Kangaroos also force partly-digested balls of grass back into their mouth. Unlike cattle, they don't spend much time chewing these "cuds."

Kangaroos chew their food for only a short time before swallowing it.

Senses alert to danger

Instead of relying on its eyes and nose, a kangaroo trusts its keen ears to warn of predators. A grazing kangaroo doesn't have to turn its head to stay alert. It can rotate each large ear in a full half-circle. When it does hear a strange noise, a kangaroo thumps the ground with one hind leg. The other kangaroos in the herd (the Australians call it a mob) flee without waiting to see what set off the alarm.

A kangaroo's eyes don't miss much. The animal can find the best grass, and it can see movement at a distance. That makes it hard to sneak up on a mob. When it's leaping, however, the kangaroo looks only straight ahead. That's probably why so many kangaroos are hit by cars; they don't look before they cross the road!

Low in brainpower

For all its size, speed, and keen senses, kangaroos aren't very smart. Naturalists rate them lower in brainpower than most placental mammals. Kangaroos fleeing from wild dogs, for example, will let themselves be trapped against a fence. In their panic, they forget that they could easily escape by jumping over the fence. Even so, these interesting marsupials have made a home for themselves in widely varied habitats.

CHAPTER TWO:

The first explorers to reach Australia found kangaroos everywhere. The many species made their homes in such varied habitats as scrub brush, grassy plains, swamps, rocky hillsides, woods, and treetops. These hardy marsupials also adjusted well to extremes of weather. Although several species are now extinct, Australia still has six times more kangaroos than it has people.

Grey kangaroos prefer a habitat of forests and open woodlands. They mostly graze on grassy areas and find shelter under the trees. This habitat exists only where there is enough winter rain to support the trees. The two main regions for greys are in eastern Australia and in the southwest. Greys are also found on the offshore island of Tasmania.

Life in the mob

A typical mob of grey kangaroos is led by an older male, called a boomer. The rest of the mob is made up of two or three females (called does) with their joeys, and several younger males. Thus, a typical mob has around ten members. The younger males stay with the mob for a while, then leave. The boomer will lead his

An older male, called a "boomer," usually leads a "mob" of kangaroos.

mob until a stronger boomer takes the does away from him.

Mobs often live peacefully side-by-side. If there is good water and grass, several hundred kangaroos may gather in a small area. When the food supply runs out, the large herds break up. The mobs drift off in different directions, each searching for a new place to graze.

The mobs also react to the weather. On very hot days, the kangaroos seek out the shade of a tree, or dig shallow holes in which to lie. During rest periods they nap, groom themselves, and roll in the dust. Most kangaroos lie on their sides, but a few roll over on their backs.

On hot days, kangaroos will search out a shady place to rest.

Even while resting, one or two males keep on the lookout for danger.

Hungry grazers, world-class leapers

Kangaroos are plant-eating animals. They graze mostly at night, favoring grasses and tree leaves. In cool weather, they may also feed during the day. Naturalists have found as many as twenty different plant varieties in a kangaroo's stomach. Eucalyptus leaves are a special favorite, but grass makes up seventy-five percent of their diet. Unlike cattle and sheep, they prefer the short grasses. A mob will pass by fields of long grasses to reach a patch of short kangaroo grass. During a drought, they feed on dry grass and straw.

Unlike cattle and sheep, kangaroos drink very little water. They obtain most of the water they need from the food they eat. If the rain stops, the adults can go a long time without water. The joeys often die during the droughts, however.

When it's grazing, the kangaroo moves slowly, nibbling on the grass as it goes. That's when it uses its five-legged gait. If it has a long way to go, the kangaroo travels in leaps of four to six feet (1.2 to 1.8 m). That works out to about ten miles per hour (16 kph). But when they're frightened, the animals may stretch

When scared, a kangaroo can leap twenty feet (6.1 m) or more.

out with leaps of twenty feet (6.1 m) or more. At top speed, the mob moves at speeds of about thirty miles per hour (48 kph). The lighter females can outrun the heavier males, unless they have joeys in their pouches.

Along with the long jump, kangaroos are world-class high jumpers. A mob can clear a six-foot (1.2 m) fence easily, but they prefer to crawl under if they can. A farmer once built a ten-foot (3 m) fence to keep them out, but the kangaroos jumped it easily! They also show their jumping ability when they're cornered. One mighty leap will carry them over the heads of their pursuers.

The kangaroo's enemies

Before humans settled in Australia, the kangaroo had few natural enemies. Eagles, Tasmanian wolves, pythons, and large lizards killed old, sick kangaroos or unprotected joeys. The biggest threat, however, was the weather. Lightning sometimes set off brushfires that burned the grass over an entire region. Drought was an even greater problem. A long drought could wipe out all the joeys born during the year.

New predators arrived with Australia's human settlers. The dingos formed packs that chased and killed single kangaroos. Rats and foxes preyed on the joeys and the smaller kangaroos. Sheep, cattle, and rabbits ruined the grass by overgrazing. Most kangaroos survived, but the toolache and brown hare wallabies are now extinct.

Kangaroos also suffer from a number of serious diseases, parasites, and insect pests. Pneumonia, a disease called "lumpy jaw," and various infections can kill them. In addition, almost all kangaroos carry worms and nematodes, but the worst pest is the sand fly. Heavy rains following a drought bring out clouds of these tiny insects. The bites of the sand flies disturb kangaroos and keep them from feeding and resting. Sometimes attack the soft areas around a kangaroo's eyes and cause it to go blind.

Timid until cornered

Kangaroos are timid and easily frightened. In most cases, they flee from danger at top speed. In their panic, they sometimes injure themselves. When cornered, they will turn and fight. Using its tail as a brace, a kangaroo kicks out with both hind legs. The sharp claws on the middle toes leave deep gashes on a careless predator. The kangaroo will also slash with its clawed forepaws, or crush its attacker in a kangaroo version of a bear hug.

Old boomers have another trick that uses their swimming ability. If a boomer is being chased by a dingo, he sometimes leaps into a river or pond. When the dingo swims in close, the boomer grabs it with his forearms. Then he holds the dingo underwater until it drowns.

It has taken naturalists a long time to collect these facts about kangaroos. Shy and always alert, kangaroos usually speed away as soon as anyone comes near. To make it harder, they're most active at night. Even so, the experts have put together a good picture of the kangaroo's life cycle.

CHAPTER THREE:

In Australia, spring arrives in October. The seasonal rains bring a new growth of thick, green grass. As the moon comes up, a mob of grey kangaroos moves slowly across a grassy clearing. The does are restless. They can mate at any season of the year, but mating activity is heaviest in the spring. The new grass means they'll have plenty of milk for their joeys.

A fight with no holds barred

The old boomer watches his does closely. He's a jealous guardian. Suddenly, his ears twitch and he coughs sharply. Another male is hopping toward the mob. The old boomer goes out to meet the intruder.

The two males drop down to all fours. They bite the fur on their chests and grunt softly. This is a kangaroo threat, but it doesn't work. Neither will back down. Now the two boomers stand erect on their hind legs. It's time for a boxing match. The old male claws at his opponent and catches him in a kangaroo hug. He looks like a wrestler trying for a take down.

All at once, the younger kangaroo breaks free. Switching to karate, each fighter launches a flurry of

Two males look like they are getting ready to fight!

A male wallaby, a close relative of the kangaroo, uses its tail in an interesting way during a fight.

powerful kicks. The old boomer connects with a double kick to the younger grey's stomach. The kick draws blood. The intruder gives up and hops away.

The old boomer returns to his mob. He grazes beside a small dark-grey doe. Soon, he begins to rub his nose against her neck. He makes soft, clucking noises. In a little while, she allows him to mate with her.

A thimble-sized joey

Five weeks later, the female is ready to give birth. She prepares her pouch by licking it clean of dirt and bits of grass. That night, a joey is born. Even if twins are born, only one will survive. The tiny female would fit easily into a large thimble. She weighs about one gram (1/25th oz.) and is less than an inch long. Hairless and blind, her muscles and blood vessels show clearly through her clear skin. She has strong forearms, but her hind legs haven't developed yet.

Instinct tells the tiny joey what to do. Her sense of smell leads her from the birth canal to the safety of the pouch. Clinging to her mother's fur with her forearms, she crawls slowly upward. This journey is the most dangerous of the joey's life. If she can't reach the pouch, or if she falls, the doe can't help her. This joey is strong and determined. After a five-minute climb, she reaches the pouch.

Life in the pouch

Once the joey is inside the pouch, she has her choice of four teats. As soon as she attaches herself to one of them, it swells up so that she can't let go. Any attempt to pull her loose would very likely kill her. A century ago, this led people to believe that a joey actually grew out of the doe's teat. Once firmly attached, the tiny joey is ready to go on with her development. She will grow in the pouch just as a placental mammal would grow in its mother's womb.

The doe is still nursing a six-month-old male. To take care of both joeys, she produces two kinds of milk. Each joey receives milk that it can digest easily. The male isn't allowed to return to the pouch, but he will go on nursing for another six months.

Soon after the joey's birth, the doe mates again. This time, however, the embryo doesn't grow in the usual way. Development is held up until the older joey is out of the pouch. Thus, a doe often has one joey at her heels, one nursing in the pouch, and one "on hold" in her body. This is nature's way of speeding up the birth process should the newborn joey die.

A first look at the world

The joey grows rapidly inside the pouch. Her hind legs develop, and her hairless body grows its first soft fur. Each day, the doe cleans the joey and the pouch with her tongue.

The joey is becoming more active. When she's about three months old, she pops her head out of the pouch

A joey takes its first look at the outside world when it is about three months old.

The joey stays close to its mother.

for the first time. Even though she's safe inside the pouch, she's easily frightened. The shadow of a circling eagle sends her back into hiding. In a little while, the shy little kangaroo peeks out again.

A month later, the doe urges the joey to leave the pouch for a while. Still timid, the joey refuses. The doe doesn't take "no" for an answer. She opens the pouch by relaxing the muscles that keep the top edge closed.

Then she bends over and tumbles the surprised joey out onto the grass.

After this sudden exit, the little joey tries out her hopping ability. Led by instinct, she nibbles on tender shoots of grass. But then a gust of wind rustles the leaves of the nearby trees. The joey turns and dives headfirst into the pouch. For a moment, her tail and hind legs stick out. Then she does a somersault and pops her head out again.

Growing up

The joey seems to grow larger day by day. Her mother holds her close each morning and licks her clean. The joey is also learning to groom herself. With tongue and claws, she cleans and brushes her own fur, just like the adult kangaroos. At a signal from the boomer, the mob moves on to a new grazing area. The joey makes the bumpy trip in the pouch. Her older brother has gone off on his own by now.

Day by day, the joey spends more time outside the pouch. If she tries to climb back when there's no real danger, the doe won't let her in. When that happens, the joey "hides" by sticking her head into the pouch! Most of the time, she's either grazing or playing with other joeys. They're all great boxers and wrestlers.

The joey also loves to wrestle with her mother. But when she tries to box with the boomer, he can't be bothered. The big male knocks her flat with a quick sweep of his forearm.

One morning in March, the joey comes close to disaster. She's feeding on leaves and grass when she hears the thump of the boomer's danger signal. Like a flash, she jumps into the pouch. The doe hops off with the mob, just ahead of a pack of dingos. But the doe can't keep up because of the heavy joey in her pouch. Without warning, she dumps the joey into some brush and speeds off. The joey springs up and hops off in another direction.

Usually, a joey who's been dumped never finds its mother again. Even if the female searches for her joey, she won't know where to look. But this joey is lucky. The dingos give up the chase, and the joey finally catches up with the mob. The doe seems happy to see her. She licks the tired joey carefully and lets her slip back into the pouch.

On her own

At ten months, the joey has outgrown the pouch. She stands forty inches (102 cm) tall and weighs twenty pounds (9 kg). The end of pouch life comes suddenly. After spending a night grazing, she tries to climb back into the pouch. The doe shoves her away. She can feed

A doe will allow the joey to nurse for about eighteen months.

from the teat, but she can't climb back into the pouch.

The months slip by. The doe still takes good care of the joey. She keeps her close at her heels most of the time. By now, the doe has another joey in her pouch. At eighteen months, the young female is almost fully grown. The doe will not allow her to nurse any longer. The joey is now a young doe, but she won't be ready to mate for another year.

The young doe is a survivor, but a cloud hangs over her future. Ranchers are bringing sheep into the territory. They will soon be complaining that the kangaroos are eating grass needed for the sheep. The old battle between wild kangaroos and their deadliest enemy is starting all over again.

People are the biggest enemies of the kangaroo.

CHAPTER FOUR:

The Dutch ship *Batavia* returned to Europe in 1629, with reports of a strange new animal. The captain said he'd seen a "type of cat" that walked on its hind legs and held its food with its forepaws. Naturalists now know that the captain was describing a Tammar wallaby.

More than a hundred years later, a British explorer reported that he'd seen an animal that carried its young in a pouch. He asked the aborigines what the animal was called. They told him it was a "kangaroo." By the 1790's, kangaroos were on display in an English zoo. People turned out by the thousands to marvel at the first marsupials seen in Europe.

A taste for "hopping mutton"

The aborigines of Australia didn't think the kangaroo was unusual. They had been hunting them with boomerangs for thousands of years. When the white settlers came, the newcomers joined in the hunt. Before long, "hopping mutton" was a main menu item at missions, cattle stations, and mining camps. Hungry farmers and miners learned to roast kangaroo loin and to make soup from the tail. The rest of the animal, they thought, was tough and tasted gamey.

With this start, Australians became more and more aware of the "roo," as they call it. They adopted the kangaroo as their national animal, and put its picture on their money, stamps, and national seal. At the same time, farmers and ranchers saw the kangaroo in only one of two ways: as a source of income or as a pest to be destroyed.

For many years, Australians killed kangaroos in the same way that Americans once killed the bison. They hunted roos with dogs and guns. At times, they even poisoned the water holes. The government put a bounty on roos, paying the hunters for every animal they killed. Hunters sometimes killed a thousand kangaroos a week.

The bounties ended in the early 1900's, but the killing went on. A market had grown for kangaroo products. The leather was exported all over the world to be made into shoes, wallets, and other products. Designers used the fur for rugs and coats. Some kangaroo fur was sold as imitation koala, because the rare koalas were protected by law. Meatpackers used the meat for sausage and pet food.

The threat of extinction

The hunting put added pressure on kangaroos that were already losing their habitats. Domestic animals packed down the soft earth and made it too hard for the small kangaroos that lived in burrows. Other species lost their living space to farms, ranches, roads, and cities.

Conservationists saw what was happening. They joined forces to put on a "save the kangaroo" campaign. Many countries, including the United States, stopped importing kangaroo hides. In Australia, the Kangaroo Protection Society worked hard to pass laws protecting the roos. They also put pressure on the government to set up national parks where wildlife can live safely.

The Kangaroo Protection Society has worked to save habitat in Australia.

Another conservation group calls itself Marsupial Mothers. These people care for joeys whose mothers have been killed by cars or hunters. Each year, thousands of roos are hit by speeding cars on Australia's open highways. The government tries to help by putting up "Kangaroo Crossing" signs to warn drivers. Marsupial Mothers also visit classrooms to educate young people about the need to save the roo.

Thousands of "roos" and other marsupials are killed every year on Australia's highways.

The killing goes on

The Australian government has responded to the conservationists. Laws now make it illegal to kill any kangaroo except reds and greys. These two species still exist in large numbers, but hunters must be licensed. Some licenses go to professional hunters, who kill roos for their hides and meat.

Other licenses go to sheepranchers. Whenever ranchers dig wells and plant grass, they create good living conditions for kangaroos. The ranchers can build fences, but they can't keep the high-jumping roos out of their pastures. When the mobs appear, ranchers ask the government for licenses to kill some of the kangaroos. Government inspectors fly over to survey the area. If they see too many roos, they grant the licenses.

So far, the laws have not stopped unlicensed killing. Some people hunt kangaroos on weekends for sport. Actually, it's not much of a sport. The kangaroo is an easy target. A roo will often leap a few times, then stop to see what the hunter is doing. Illegal hunters, called poachers, kill an even larger number of kangaroos. The Wild Life Service tries to catch the poachers, but Australia is too large to patrol easily.

Experts guess that Australians are killing a million kangaroos a year. But they also admit that the roo population is still increasing. Despite all that hunters can do, the big kangaroos are more than holding their own.

CHAPTER FIVE:

The kangaroo hunter looked unhappy. He shielded his eyes from the sun and squinted at the tall woman.

"Dr. Harris, are you sure you want to go with me?" Kelly asked for the third time. He was a small, rugged man, dressed in dusty workclothes. "I'm going out to shoot roos, and I won't take it kindly if you try to stop me."

The woman nodded. "I'm here in Queensland to study marsupials," she said. "Part of my job is to look at the effect of hunting on the kangaroos. I know you're a licensed hunter. I don't like what you're doing, but I understand it."

Hunters go where the roos are

The sun was setting when Kelly helped the naturalist into his truck. It was a big pickup with heavy-duty springs. As the truck roared out of town, Dr. Harris asked about the truck's spotlight.

"That's to dazzle the roos," Kelly said. "Without it, they'd be gone before I could get close enough to get a shot at them."

Meat hunters have not harmed the populations of either grey (pictured) or red kangaroos.

The truck turned off the gravel road and bumped across the dusty plains. "We've got another forty miles to go," he told the naturalist. "There's been rain up in the basin. The roos will be coming in tonight to eat the new grass and fill up on the water."

Night was closing in on the dry, brush-covered plain. At first glance, it looked like a lifeless land. But Dr. Harris knew that many marsupials had adapted to these conditions.

A hard way to make a living

"Do you make a good living as a hunter?" she asked.

Kelly's laugh was harsh. "The blokes at the packing house pay less than ten cents (US) a pound!" he said. "The pet food makers and the leather factories make all the money. They export to Asia and Europe. A lot of Germans are wearing kangaroo-hide boots from the roos I've shot."

Dr. Harris frowned. "Then why do you do it?" she wondered.

"Look at it this way," Kelly said. "A kangaroo eats about as much grass as sheep. It chews the grass down close to the roots, killing lots of it. Everytime I shoot a roo, some rancher can keep another sheep. Australia needs more sheep. We sell the mutton and wool for British pounds and Japanese yen. The money goes to buy imported cars, computers, and other equipment."

Dr. Harris knew Kelly's argument wasn't entirely true. Kangaroos often feed on grasses that sheep won't touch. But she decided not to argue the point. Aloud, she said, "Why do you do good deeds for sheep ranchers if you're so poorly paid?"

Kelly sighed. "I don't have much choice. My dad tried to run sheep here. Then the drought dried everything up. His sheep died, along with millions of others. It was hunt roos or starve."

"I know you only get twelve inches (30 cm) of rain a year," Dr. Harris agreed. "That's barely enough to graze sheep."

"Parts of the outback may go a hundred years without rain," Kelly said. "Then the rains come, and leave a lake as big as Belgium."

The hunt begins

The truck was weaving its way through a tangle of underbrush and eucalyptus trees. The headlights were reflected in the eyes of a thousand small marsupials.

Kelly put the truck in low gear and inched down a hill. At the bottom was a hot spring where water bubbled out of the ground. Kelly turned and followed the stream.

Suddenly, the kangaroos were there. They looked like grey ghosts in the headlights. Some of them jumped back into the darkness. But others stayed and stared into the lights. Kelly put on the brakes and grabbed his rifle. A moment later, he was firing. Dr. Harris covered her ears as the kangaroo hunter pulled the trigger again and again.

When the last roo had fled, Kelly drove forward and repeated the process. Finally, the spotlight showed nothing but empty brush. Kelly turned around and picked up the dead roos. Dr. Harris counted fifteen bodies. Kelly gutted the animals with a knife. Then he hung them from hooks welded to a frame above the bed of the truck.

It's time for a cup of tea

Dr. Harris made notes on the sex and condition of each dead roo. She was pleased to see that Kelly didn't shoot does with a joey at heel. Even so, she felt saddened by the night's work.

By dawn, the truck held twenty-eight kangaroos. Kelly guessed that they'd weigh in at about four thousand pounds (1,814 kg). "By the time I pay my costs," he said, "I'll clear about five American dollars for each one."

Dr. Harris had started out the day ready to hate Kelly. Now she wasn't sure what she felt. The hunter believed he was doing honest work. One thing was certain. For all the hard work, he wasn't getting rich hunting kangaroos.

"Okay, Kelly," she said. "I've seen all I want to see. Take me back to town and I'll buy you a cup of tea."

In spite of all that people have done to them, most members of the kangaroo family are doing very well.

MAP:

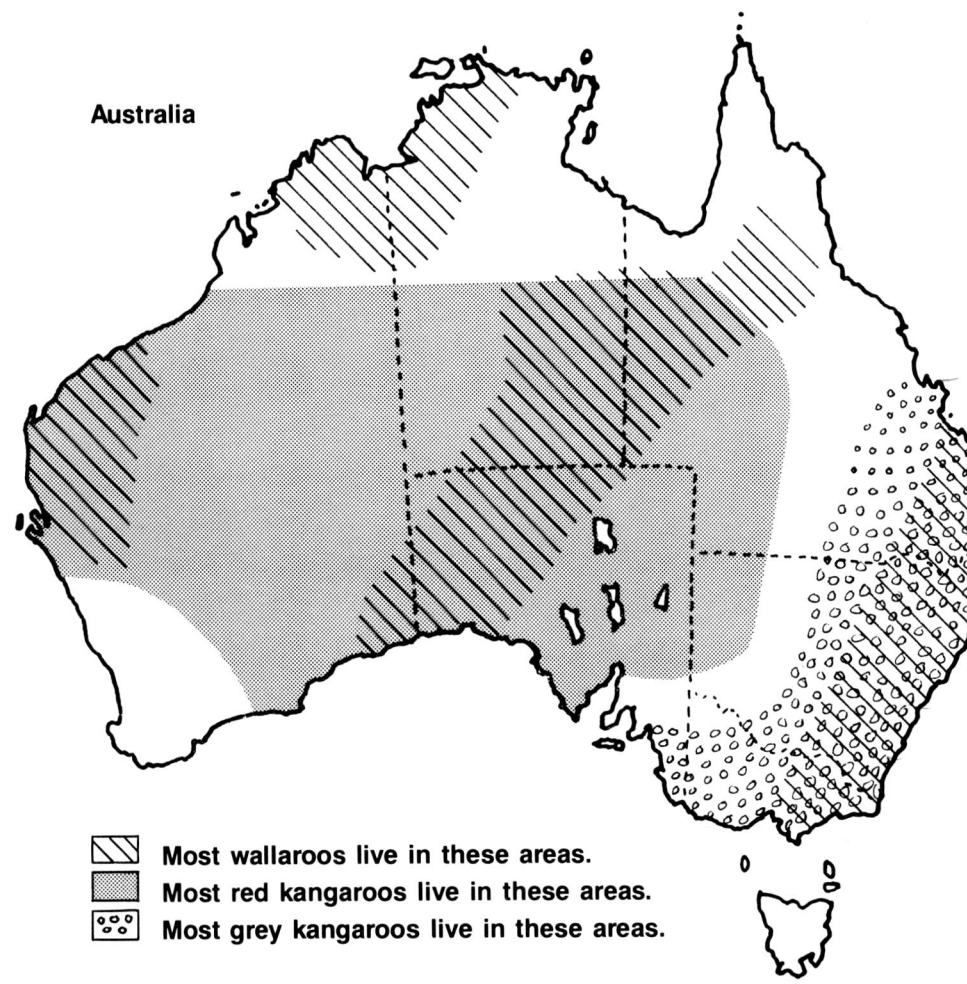

Australia

◩ Most wallaroos live in these areas.
▨ Most red kangaroos live in these areas.
▧ Most grey kangaroos live in these areas.

INDEX/GLOSSARY:

ABORIGINES 7, 35 — *The original human inhabitants of Australia.*

BOOMER 16, 17, 18, 22, 23, 26, 31, 32 — *An adult male kangaroo.*

BOOMERANG 35 — *A flat, wooden weapon which curves back to the user's hand after it's been thrown.*

BURROW 37 — *A hole or tunnel dug in the ground and used as a home by some small marsupials.*

CONSERVATIONIST 37, 38, 39 — *Someone who believes in protecting our natural resources.*

DINGO 7, 21, 22, 32 — *A wild dog that lives in Australia.*

DOE 16, 18, 23, 27, 28, 30, 32, 33, 34, 44 — *An adult female kangaroo.*

DROUGHT 19, 21, 43 — *A long period with little or no rain.*

EMBRYO 28 — *An unborn animal during the early stages of growth.*

HABITAT 8, 9, 10, 15, 16, 36, 37 — *The place where an animal makes its home.*

JOEY 4, 11, 16, 19, 20, 21, 23, 27, 28, 29, 30, 31, 32, 33, 38, 44 — *A young male or female kangaroo.*

MARSUPIALS 6, 7, 8, 11, 15, 16, 35, 38, 40, 42, 43 — *Mammals whose young complete their development in the female's pouch rather than inside her body.*

MOB 15, 16, 17, 18, 19, 20, 23, 26, 31, 32, 39 — *A herd of kangaroos.*

NATURALIST 7, 15, 19, 22, 35, 40, 42 — *A scientist who studies animals and plants.*

PARASITE 21 — *Any insect, bacteria, or worm that lives in and feeds on a kangaroo or other animal.*

PLACENTA 6 — *A sack within a female mammal's body that provides the nourishment needed by a developing embryo.*

PLACENTAL MAMMALS 4, 7, 15, 28 — *Mammals whose young reach full development before they're born.*

POUCH 4, 5, 6, 20, 27, 28, 30, 31, 33, 35 — *The "pocket" on the outside of the mother's stomach in which a marsupial lives while it completes its development.*

PREDATORS 15, 21, 22 — *Animals that live by preying on other animals.*

TEATS 27, 28, 33 — *The doe's nipples. Joeys suck on the doe's teats to obtain milk.*

READ AND ENJOY THE SERIES:

If you would like to know more about all kinds of wildlife, you should take a look at the other books in this series.

You'll find books on bald eagles and other birds. Books on alligators and other reptiles. There are books about deer and other big-game animals. And there are books about sharks and other creatures that live in the ocean.

In all of the books you will learn that life in the wild is not easy. But you will also learn what people can do to help wildlife survive. So read on!